KILL/MARRY/FUC

KILL/MARRY/FUC

BY **SARAH HUBER**
MARK BATTY PUBLISHER, NEW YORK

Library of Congress Control Number: 2011924597
Printed and bound in Hong Kong through Asia Pacific Offset
10 9 8 7 6 5 4 3 2 1   First edition

This edition © 2011
Mark Batty Publisher
68 Jay Street, Suite 410
Brooklyn, NY 11201
www.markbattypublisher.com

Distributed outside North America by:
Thames & Hudson Ltd
181A High Holborn
London WC1V 7QX
United Kingdom
Tel: 00 44 20 7845 5000
Fax: 00 44 20 7845 5055
www.thameshudson.co.uk

ISBN: 978-1-9356133-7-4

Editor: Buzz Poole
Design: Damian Browning - www.thegravy.co.uk
Production: Christopher D Salyers
Illustrations: Mat Bartlett - www.matbartlett.co.uk

IT'S A GAME.

KMF IS A FORCED CHOICE GAME IN WHICH THE PLAYER(S) ARE GIVEN A GROUP OF THREE PEOPLE, PLACES OR THINGS THAT MAY OR MAY NOT REFLECT THE PLAYERS' SEXUAL INTERESTS. REGARDLESS, OF THE THREE, THEY MUST CHOOSE WHICH ONE THEY'D KILL, WHICH ONE THEY'D MARRY AND WHICH ONE THEY'D FUCK. THEN, EXPLAIN WHY.

PLAY IT.

THE BLONDES

CHARLIZE THERON

FACT

Charlize was named after her father, Charles. When she was fifteen, her father attacked her mother and her mother shot and killed him in self-defense.

SCARLETT JOHANSSON

FACT

At thirteen, Scarlett lost the lead role in *The Parent Trap* to Lindsay Lohan. She also auditioned for the role of Karen in *Mean Girls* but lost out to Amanda Seyfried.

BLAKE LIVELY

FACT

Blake's mother sent her to first grade three years early because her older brother didn't want to go alone. She was removed after a few weeks after the school reported that Blake was "slow" and slept a lot, unaware she was only three.

FUN FACT
There have been 48 *Sports Illustrated* swimsuit issues since 1964:
- 24 Blonde cover girls – average annual return of Dow 10.0%, S&P 10.9%
- 20 Brunette cover girls – average annual return of Dow 2.2%, S&P 2.3%
- 3 covers with multiple models with different hair color
- 1 cover with a redhead

ANGELINA JOLIE

QUOTE

"You're young, you're drunk, you're in bed, you have knives; shit happens."

MILA KUNIS

QUOTE

"Blondes definitely do not have more fun. Trust me."

MEGAN FOX

QUOTE

"I'm horrible to live with. I don't clean. My clothes end up wherever I take them off. I forget to flush the toilet. Friends will tell me, 'Megan, you totally pinched a loaf in my toilet and didn't flush.'"

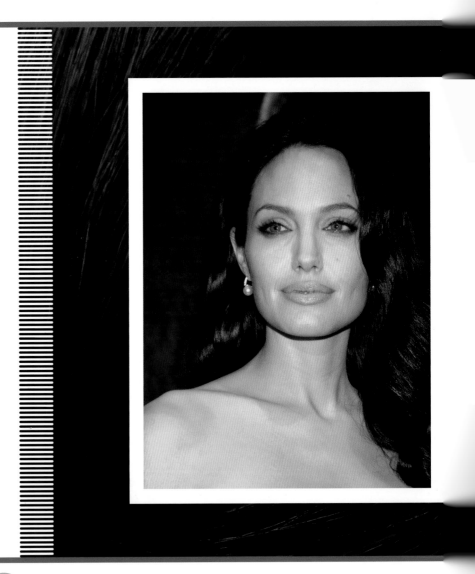

THE BRUNETTES

KILL/MARRY/F

THE GINGERS

DANNY BONADUCE

FACT
For over twenty years, he studied martial arts with Chuck Norris.

CARROT TOP

FACT
Carrot Top's father, rocket scientist Larry Thompson, worked on the Gemini and Apollo missions.

DAVID CARUSO

FACT
His three divorces are recognized by the federal government but same-sex marriages are not.

THE CITIES

CHICAGO, IL

Population: 2.7 million

FACT

According to local legend, the Smurfit-Stone Building, or the "Vagina Building," was designed as a feminist response to the otherwise phallic skyline.

NEW YORK, NY

Population: 8.5 million

FACT

It takes 75,000 trees to print a Sunday edition of the *New York Times*.

LOS ANGELES

Population: 3.9 million

FACT

The Clippers suck.

SHANNEN DOHERTY

Brenda Walsh

FACT

While on *90210*, making $17,500 per week, Shannen had her wages garnished by the California United Bank for writing bad checks totaling nearly $32,000.

JENNIE GARTH

Kelly Taylor

FACT

Auditioned for the role of Kelly Kapowski on *Saved by the Bell* but lost out to her future friend and *90210* co-star, Tiffani Amber Thiessen.

TORI SPELLING

Donna Martin

FACT

Got a nose job after her pet parrot bit her.

THE CLASS OF '93

LUKE PERRY

Dylan McKay

FACT
Originally auditioned for the
role of Steve Sanders.

IAN ZIERING

Steve Sanders

FACT
Ian's father, Paul Ziering, was
Chelsea Handler's Hebrew teacher.

JASON PRIESTLY

Brandon Walsh

FACT
Slept with Shannen Doherty.

THE 3 OF SPADE

PAMELA ANDERSON
Scott Baio's Ex-Girlfriend

CARMEN ELECTRA
Scott Baio's Ex-Girlfriend

HEATHER LOCKLEAR
Scott Baio's Ex-Girlfriend

SPOUSES
Tommy Lee (1995-1998)
Kid Rock (2006-2007)
Rick Saloman (2007-2008)

SPOUSES
Dennis Rodman (1998-1999)
Dave Navarro (2003-2007)

SPOUSES
Tommy Lee (1986-1993)
Richie Sambora (1994-2007)

KILL/MARRY/FU

Albert Einstein receives the Nobel Prize in Physics.

Charlie Chaplin releases his first full-length movie, *The Kid.*

King Tut's tomb is discovered.

BETTY WHITE
January 17, 1922

1920 | 1921 | 1922 | 1923 | 1924

Babe Ruth joins the New York Yankees for $100,000 ($1,100,000 in current terms).

Coco Chanel introduces Chanel No. 5. Today, a bottle is sold every thirty seconds and generates sales of $100 million a year.

BOB BARKER
December 12, 1923

The IBM corporation is founded.

IBM

THE '20s

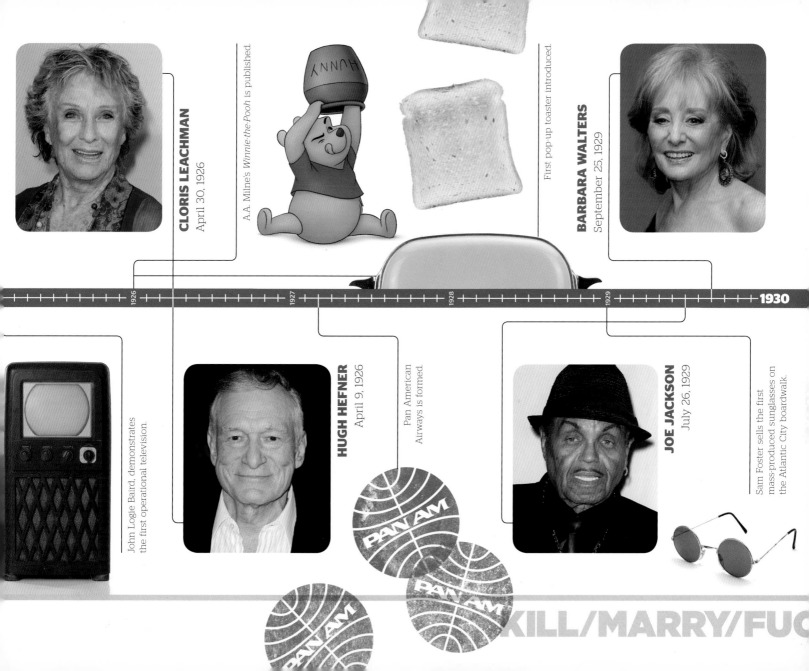

CLORIS LEACHMAN
April 30, 1926

A.A. Milne's *Winnie-the-Pooh* is published.

First pop-up toaster introduced.

BARBARA WALTERS
September 25, 1929

1926   1927   1928   1929   **1930**

John Logie Baird, demonstrates the first operational television.

HUGH HEFNER
April 9, 1926

Pan American Airways is formed.

JOE JACKSON
July 26, 1929

Sam Foster sells the first mass-produced sunglasses on the Atlantic City boardwalk.

KILL/MARRY/FU

THE HAPPY HOUR

WINE

FACT

When Johnny Depp was engaged to Winona Ryder, he had "Winona Forevor" tattooed on his arm. After the couple split in 1993, he had it changed to read "Wino Forever."

LIQUOR

FACT

With only thirty-two letters, one of the shortest sentences in the English language to use every letter of the alphabet is, "pack my box with five dozen liquor jugs."

BEER

FACT

In an effort to encourage home consumption, the six pack of beer was introduced in 1938. Numerous studies found that six cans were the ideal weight for the average housewife to carry home from the store.

FUN FACT
Prohibition began on January 16, 1920. It lasted 13 years, 10 months, 19 days, 17 hours, 32 minutes, and 30 seconds. The ban was rescinded on December 5, 1933, at 3:32 pm.

KILL/MARRY/FUC

THE CURSED

REESE WITHERSPOON

. . . .

Married in 1999
Won in 2006
Split in 2006

QUOTE

"You make more money than I do. Go ahead."

- Ryan Phillippe, handing Reese the envelope when
the couple jointly presented at the 2002 Oscars

KATE WINSLET

. . . .

Married in 2003
Won in 2009
Split in 2010

QUOTE

"We are very happy, but obviously
there is a cathartic aspect of making
a movie about a bad marriage."

- Sam Mendes on *Revolutionary Road*

SANDRA BULLOCK

. . . .

Married in 2005
Won in 2010
Split in 2010

QUOTE

"It's a once-in-a-lifetime opportunity to support
my wife and her work. She does it all the time
for me. She goes to Mexico, to the desert, to the
hospital - a lot - to support me and my work. The
least I can do is put on a suit and support her."

- Jesse James, Oscar night

FUN FACTS
According to a study done by researchers at the University of Toronto and Carnegie Mellon University...
• There have been 751 Academy Award nominees in the Best Actor and Actress categories between 1936 and 2010.
• The median marriage duration of Best Actress winners is 4.30 years. It is 9.51 years for non-winners.
• Best Actress winners have a 63% chance that their marriages end sooner than non-winners.
• By contrast, the median marriage duration for Best Actor winners is 12.66 years and is 11.97 for non-winners.

KILL/MARRY/FUC

CHRIS BROWN

QUOTE

"My mother taught me to treat a lady respectfully."

JOHN MAYER

QUOTE

"My dick is sort of like a white supremicist. I've got a Benetton heart and a fuckin' David Duke cock."

BEN ROETHLISBERGER

QUOTE

"I like being the hunter rather than the hunted."

xx love Breezy xx

THE ROMANTICS

Love John + David xx

LOVE BIG BEN X

KILL/MARRY/FU

THE ONE NIGHT STAND

LINDSAY LOHAN

QUOTE

"People go to college to find who they are as a person and find what they want to do in life, and I kind of already know that so it would be like I'd be taking a step back or something."

BRITNEY SPEARS

QUOTE

"I've never really wanted to go to Japan. Simply because I don't like eating fish. And I know that's very popular out there in Africa."

PARIS HILTON

QUOTE

"One of my heroes is Barbie. She may not do anything, but she always looks great doing it."

KILL/MARRY/FU

AMANDA PEET

Columbia '94

FACT

While studying history, she was convinced to audition for the renowned acting coach, Uta Hagen, who inspired her to become an actress.

RASHIDA JONES

Harvard '97

FACT

Initially went to study law but the O.J. Simpson trial changed her mind. She graduated with degrees in both religion and philosophy.

NATALIE PORTMAN

Harvard '03

FACT

After graduating with a degree in psychology, she went on to take graduate courses at the Hebrew University in Jerusalem.

THE IVY LEAGUE

MATTHEW FOX

Columbia '89

FACT
His plans were to work on Wall Street. He majored in economics, played football, and is a member of Phi Gamma Delta.

JOHN KRASINSKI

Brown '01

FACT
Taught English in Costa Rica before entering Brown and getting a degree in playwriting.

JAMES FRANCO

Yale

FACT
Currently majoring in English and was underwhelming at the Oscars.

KILL/MARRY/FU

THE STONERS

KEITH RICHARDS

....

QUOTE

"I've never had a problem with drugs.
I've had problems with the police."

BILL MAHER

....

QUOTE

"I'm getting tired of being treated like a criminal
or a second class citizen by people who through
their preference for liquor or pills for mood alteration
show not a superiority of taste but an inferiority."

SNOOP DOGG

....

QUOTE

"When I'm no longer rapping, I want to open up
an ice cream parlor and call myself Scoop Dogg."

Al Capone jailed for income tax evasion.

DEBBIE REYNOLDS
April 1, 1932

Beer is legalized in the United States, eight months before the full repeal of Prohibition.

SOPHIA LOREN

1930 | 1931 | 1932 | 1933 | 1934

3M invents Scotch Tape to help people "make do" during the Great Depression.

SCOTCH
BRAND
Cellulose
TAPE
1 Roll - ½ x 792 Inches
TRANSPARENT

SEAN CONNERY
August 25, 1930

Boris Karloff stars as the monster in *Frankenstein*.

First sighting of the Loch Ness monster.

Donald Duck appears for the first time in *The Wise Little Hen*.

THE '30s

Parker Brothers releases Monopoly.

Ruth Wakefield, owner of the Toll House Inn, accidentally invents the first chocolate chip cookie.

JANE FONDA
December 21, 1937

Gone with the Wind premieres.

"FRANKLY MY DEAR, I DON'T GIVE A DAMN"

1936 · 1937 · 1938 · 1939 · **1940**

ROBERT REDFORD
August 18, 1936

Vernon Rudolph opens the first Krispy Kreme Doughnuts store in Winston-Salem, NC.

Krispy Kreme
DOUGHNUTS®

WARREN BEATTY
March 30, 1937

The Fair Labor Standards Act of 1938 creates the minimum wage and sets it at 25 cents an hour.

The first pair of nylon stockings is sold in Wilmington, DE.

KILL/MAR

BATMAN

Bruce Wayne

POWERS

High human strength, great agility, master of martial arts,
genius level intelligence, fantastic observational skills,
and knows how to use electronics. Is also a billionaire.

SUPERMAN

Clark Kent

POWERS

Super human strength, speed, stamina, longevity, super
breath, x-ray vision, super sense of smell and hearing,
fluent in most languages, flawless memory, and can fly.

SPIDERMAN

Peter Parker

POWERS

Super human strength, speed, great agility, great reflexes
and balance, genius level intelligence, can sense danger,
can cling to most surfaces, can shoot spider webs from
his wrist, and has a high tolerance for drugs and alcohol.

THE HEROES

KILL/MARRY/FUC

THE MOVERS

BILL GATES

Forbes US rank: #1

NET WORTH	$56 billion
SOURCE	Microsoft
AGE	55
RESIDENCE	Medina, Washington
EDUCATION	Harvard University drop out
MARITAL STATUS	Married, three children

MARK ZUCKERBERG

Forbes US rank: #19

NET WORTH	$13.5 billion
SOURCE	Facebook
AGE	26
RESIDENCE	Palo Alto, California
EDUCATION	Harvard University drop out
MARITAL STATUS	Single

STEVE JOBS

Forbes US rank: #34

NET WORTH	$8.3 billion
SOURCE	Apple, Pixar
AGE	56
RESIDENCE	Palo Alto, California
EDUCATION	Reed College drop out
MARITAL STATUS	Married, four children

KILL/MARRY/FUC

THE SHAKERS

MICHAEL J. FOX

Diagnosed with Parkinson's in 1991

FACT

Michael's real middle name is Andrew but when he went to join the Screen Actor's Guild, there was already a Michael Fox. He changed his middle initial to J because he didn't want to be referred to as Michael A. Fox.

QUOTE

"People always ask me if I say to myself 'Why Me?' and I tell them, 'Why not me?'"

MUHAMMAD ALI

Diagnosed with Parkinson's in 1984

FACT

Ali's great-grandfather was Irish. Abe Grady emigrated from Ennis, Ireland, and settled in Kentucky in the 1860s. Ali visited his ancestral home in 2009 where he was proclaimed the town's first "freeman," an honor granting several privileges, most notably, free parking.

QUOTE

"My toughest fight was with my first wife."

OZZY OSBOURNE

Diagnosed with Parkin Syndrome in 2005

FACT

While many people, including Ozzy himself, believed that his diagnosis was a result of his hard partying ways, Parkin Syndrome is a genetic condition. With similar symptoms to Parkinson's, it is shared by his grandmother, mother, and aunt.

QUOTE

"Could be worse...I could be Sting."

JENNIFER LOPEZ

FACT

In 2004, while playing the $1 slots at the Borgata Casino in Atlantic City, her mother won a $2.4 million jackpot.

JENNIFER ANISTON

FACT

While Aniston and Brad Pitt were together, she helped him acquire the rights for the story of Daniel Pearl's wife in *A Mighty Heart* and was originally slated to play the role of Mariane. Angelina Jolie got the part instead.

JENNIFER GARNER

FACT

Garner married her *Felicity* costar, Scott Foley. She left him for her *Alias* costar Michael Vartan and then left him for her *Daredevil* costar Ben Affleck.

THE JENNIFERS

KILL/MARRY/FUC

THE OCEAN'S THREE

MATT DAMON

Linus Caldwell

FACT

Mark Wahlberg was originally offered the role of Linus but he turned it down to do *Planet of the Apes* instead.

GEORGE CLOONEY

Danny Ocean

FACT

Auditioned five times for Ridley Scott for the role of J.D. in *Thelma & Louise* but lost out to Brad Pitt.

BRAD PITT

Rusty Ryan

FACT

The scene around the Bellagio fountain where everyone walks away was somewhat improvised. Steven Soderbergh wanted Pitt to leave first and then the other actors were told to just leave in whatever order felt natural.

FUN FACT
Danny Glover was supposed to play Bernie Mac's role and Luke and Owen Wilson were supposed to play the brothers played by Casey Affleck and Scott Caan. All three chose to do *The Royal Tenenbaums* instead.

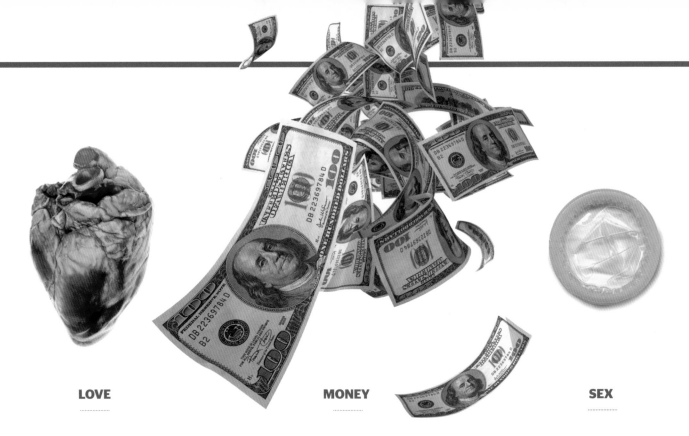

LOVE

FACT

Ancient Egyptians believed that the vein of love ran from the fourth finger of the left hand directly to the heart, hence the wedding ring tradition.

MONEY

FACT

Three quarters, four dimes, and four pennies ($1.19) is the largest amount of money you can have in coins without being able to make change for a dollar.

SEX

FACT

According to sex shops, the most popular flavor of edible underwear is cherry. The least popular is chocolate.

THE PRIORITIES

YOUR FIRST KISS

FACT
Approximately two-thirds of people tip their head to the right when they kiss. Some experts speculate this preference starts in the womb.

YOUR FIRST TIME

FACT
June is the most common month when Americans lose their virginity.

YOUR FIRST LOVE

FACT
Scientists suggest that most people will fall in love approximately seven times before marriage.

The first McDonald's is opened in San Bernardino, CA by brothers Richard and Maurice McDonald.

Orson Welles' film *Citizen Kane* premieres in New York City.

BARBRA STREISAND
April 24, 1942

Naval engineer Richard James invents the Slinky.

1940 | 1941 | 1942 | 1943 | 1944

Bugs Bunny makes his official debut in *A Wild Hare.*

MARTIN SCORSESE
November 17, 1942

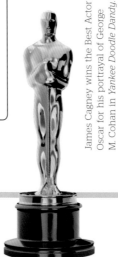

James Cagney wins the Best Actor Oscar for his portrayal of George M. Cohan in *Yankee Doodle Dandy.*

GEORGE LUCAS
May 14, 1944

THE '40s

BETTE MIDLER
December 1, 1945

National Basketball
Association founded.

NBA

CHER
May 20, 1946

Hells Angels Motorcycle Club
formed in Fontana, California.

HELLS ANGELS MC

1946

1947

1948

1949

1950

Anne Frank dies of
typhus while at
the Bergen-Belsen
concentration camp
just a few weeks before
the camp is liberated
by British troops.

STEVEN SPIELBERG
December 18, 1946

A spacecraft and its alien occupants
are allegedly recovered at a crash
site in the Roswell UFO incident.

The first Polaroid
camera launched.

Scrabble is introduced
by James Brunot.

H₄ I₁

M₃ A₁

M₃

A₁

KILL/MARRY

RYAN GOSLING

FACT

In the band's formative years, A.J. McLean tried to get Gosling to audition for the Backstreet Boys. Fortunately, he passed.

RYAN PHILLIPPE

FACT

As young up-and-comers, Phillippe hung out with Breckin Meyer and Seth Green. "We would break into malls at night. We'd go on top of buildings and unplug things." The three now own a production company together called Lucid Films.

RYAN REYNOLDS

FACT

Reynolds developed a fear of flying after a skydiving incident where his chute failed to open properly. "I had to pull the reserve. I got down on the ground, removed my urine-spackled jumpsuit and threw it at the guy and got in my car and drove extremely slowly home. It was the worst."

THE RYANS

KILL/MARRY/FU

HALLE BERRY – February 23, 2000

It was reported that Berry ran a red light, hit a twenty-seven year-old woman's car, and then sped off. The woman filed suit and the case was eventually settled out of court. Berry was charged with a misdemeanor, received three years probation, 200 hours of community service, and a $13,500 fine. Cops then confirmed that Berry was involved in a similar incident three years prior but the parties settled out of court and no charges were filed. In 2007, two days after announcing her pregnancy, Berry crashed her car into a wall.

REBECCA GAYHEART – June 13, 2001

According to police, Gayheart came upon vehicles that had stopped for a boy who was crossing the street. She drove around the stationary cars and struck the nine year-old boy who died the next day. The boy's family filed suit, which was settled out of court. Gayheart pled no contest to vehicular manslaughter, received three years probation, one year suspended license, a $2,800 fine, and 750 hours of community service. In October of that same year, Gayheart flipped her car into two parked cars. Gayheart's parents spoke out saying that they no longer wanted their daughter to drive.

BRANDY NORWOOD – December 30, 2006

According to police, Norwood was driving on an LA freeway when she failed to notice the vehicles in front of her had slowed down. She crashed into a thirty-eight year-old woman's car, causing the vehicle to cross lanes and get hit by two additional cars. The woman died the next day. No charges were filed. However, five separate lawsuits were filed against the singer. One by the victim's parents for $50 million, one by the victim's husband, who rejected an offer of $1.2 million, one on behalf of her two sons, and two from separate drivers involved in the crash.

Halle

THE BAD DRIVERS

Rebecca

Brandy

KILL/MARRY/FUC

MILKY WAY

Life's better the Milky Way

FACT

Created in 1923, it was the first filled chocolate bar that was commercially distributed.
It was named after the popular malted milkshakes at the time, not the Earth's galaxy.

SNICKERS

Don't let hunger happen to you

FACT

Introduced in 1930, the Snickers candy bar was named after founders Frank and Ethel Mars' favorite horse.

THREE MUSKETEERS

A lighter way to enjoy chocolate

FACT

Introduced in 1932, the package originally included three pieces: one chocolate, one strawberry, and one vanilla, hence the name.

THE CANDY

M&M's

Melts in your mouth, not in your hand

FACT

M&M's were created by the son of
Frank Mars and the son of the Hershey's
president, Bruce Murrie. The name
is short for Mars & Murrie.

SKITTLES

Taste the rainbow

FACT

It takes approximately 8 hours to complete
the candy coating on the outside of the
fruit center and more that 200,000,000
Skittles are produced each day.

REESE'S PIECES

There's no wrong way to eat a Reese's

FACT

Universal Studios originally wanted
to use M&M's in E.T. but Mars said no.
Hershey's, who hadn't advertised
since the 1930s, said yes.

APPLEBEE'S

est. 1980 in Atlanta, GA

FACT

With over 1900 Applebee's in 49 states (all but Hawaii) and sixteen countries, they're the largest casual-dining concept in the world.

OLIVE GARDEN

est. 1982 in Orlando, FL

FACT

There are over 670 locations nationwide and the average annual sales per restaurant is 4.9 million. The restaurant was originally developed by General Mills, Inc.

RED LOBSTER

est. 1968 in Lakeland, FL

FACT

There are over 680 locations in the US & Canada. They serve more than 395 million cheese biscuits each year or 1.1 million per day.

THE CHAINS

MCDONALD'S

est. 1940 in San Bernadino, CA

FACT

There are over 32,000 locations worldwide. Ronald McDonald is called Donald McDonald in Japan because there is no clear "r" sound in Japanese.

WENDY'S

est. 1969 in Columbus, OH

FACT

In order to open up a new Wendy's franchise, you need to have a minimum net worth of $1,000,000 and a minimum of $500,000 in liquid assets.

BURGER KING

est. 1953 in Jacksonville, FL

FACT

They are the world's second largest burger chain with over 12,200 locations. Burger King was privately held for fifty-two years before going public in 2006.

KILL/MARRY/FUC

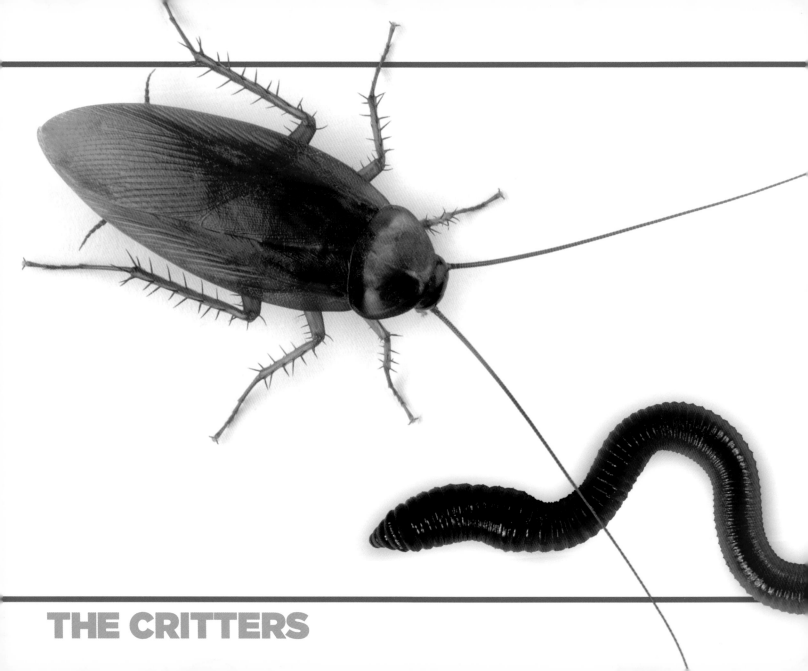

THE CRITTERS

COCKROACH

....

FACT

A cockroach can run up to three miles an hour, live up to a month without food, and live up to a week with its head cut off - in which case it only dies from not being able to drink water.

WORM

....

FACT

Earthworms can control the volume of their ejaculation depending upon the quality of their mate. For example, if they sense their mate is not a virgin, they will triple the amount of sperm they release in order to drown out the sperm of any previous mate.

SPIDER

....

FACT

There's a fascinating study on how a spider spins its web when it's under the influence of different drugs. You should Google it. Spiders on speed spin their webs "with great gusto, but apparently without much planning leaving large holes." Spiders on marijuana "made a reasonable stab at spinning webs but appeared to lose concentration about half-way through."

THE QUITTERS

MACKENZIE PHILLIPS

·················

Celebrity Rehab Season 3

QUOTE

"I woke up that night from a blackout to
find myself having sex with my own father."

JANICE DICKINSON

·················

Celebrity Rehab Season 4

QUOTE

"As the saying goes, I want to be
the best looking corpse there is."

HEIDI FLEISS

·················

Celebrity Rehab Season 3

QUOTE

"Look, I had the party, did the party, threw
the party, was the party. I'm partied out."

Shirley Temple announces her retirement from show business.

The first KFC franchise was opened by Colonel Harland Sanders and Pete Harman in South Salt Lake, Utah.

CHRISTIE BRINKLEY
February 2, 1954

Hasbro launches Mr. Potato Head. The original kit didn't include a body so parents had to provide their own potato.

1950 | **1951** | **1952** | **1953** | **1954**

Charles M. Schulz's *Peanuts* comic strip debuts.

First edition of J.D. Salinger's *The Catcher in the Rye* is published. Over 65 million copies have been sold to date.

PIERCE BROSNAN
May 16, 1953

Hugh Hefner publishes the first issue of *Playboy*. It sells 54,175 copies at 50¢ each.

THE '50s

SHARON STONE
March 10, 1958

MICHELLE PFEIFFER
April 29, 1958

James Dean is killed in a car crash at a highway junction near Cholame, CA. Dean is just twenty-four years old.

MOTOWN®

Motown Records is founded by Berry Gordy.

| | 1956 | | 1957 | | 1958 | | 1959 | | **1960** |

MEL GIBSON
January 3, 1956

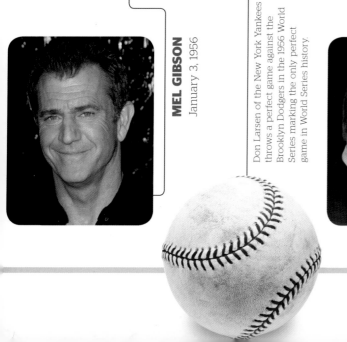

Don Larsen of the New York Yankees throws a perfect game against the Brooklyn Dodgers in the 1956 World Series marking the only perfect game in World Series history.

ALEC BALDWIN
April 3, 1958

Commissioned by the Campaign for Nuclear Disarmament, the peace symbol is designed by Gerald Holtom.

KILLA   FUC

ELLEN DEGENERES

FACT

Before getting her start in comedy, she worked as a vacuum cleaner saleswoman, an oyster shucker, and as a waitress at T.G.I. Friday's.

OPRAH WINFREY

FACT

Her name was supposed to be Orpah after Ruth's sister-in-law in the Bible but was misspelled Oprah on her birth certificate. They just went with it.

TYRA BANKS

FACT

Was the first African American woman to grace the covers of *GQ*, the *Sports Illustrated Swimsuit Issue*, and the Victoria's Secret catalog. Also has an extreme fear of dolphins.

THE TALK TITANS

JAY LENO

FACT

His famous chin is the result of a genetic disorder called mandibular prognathism in which the lower jaw outgrows the upper jaw. It's also called Habsburg Jaw after the royal family who all had similar chins thanks to inbreeding.

CONAN O'BRIEN

FACT

While at Harvard, Conan was president of the *Harvard Lampoon*, a humor magazine. At the same time, former NBC president, Jeff Zucker, who fired Conan from the *Tonight Show*, was president of the rival publication, the *Harvard Crimson*.

DAVID LETTERMAN

FACT

Margaret Mary Ray, who suffered from schizophrenia, was arrested eight times for stalking Letterman. After serving time in prison, she briefly directed her attention to astronaut Story Musgrave before throwing herself in front on an oncoming train.

KILL/MARRY/FUC

MUSTARD

FACT

More than 1,600 gallons (over two million individual packets) are consumed in one year at Yankee Stadium.

MAYONNAISE

FACT

The Kardashians put mayonnaise on their vagina because it "makes it shine like the top of the Chrysler Building."

KETCHUP

FACT

The original ketchup didn't contain tomatoes. It was a mixture of anchovies, walnuts, mushrooms, and kidney beans.

THE CONDIMENTS

FORK

FACT

Around 1000 AD, the Catholic church in Italy banned the use of forks because it was considered an assault on God's intentions for fingers.

SPOON

FACT

Paterson, NJ, is home to a spoon museum with more than 5,000 spoons from every state and almost every country in the world.

KNIFE

FACT

Chuck Norris once got in a knife fight... the knife lost.

THE JESSICAS

JESSICA ALBA

QUOTE

"I thought it was my job to give all the boys their first kiss."

JESSICA BIEL

QUOTE

"I've never gotten to do romantic comedy like most of the girls. Maybe because I'm fit, people assume that I'm not funny?"

JESSICA SIMPSON

QUOTE

"My mom was really worried I'd grow up looking strange, so every night before I went to bed, she'd pull my legs and stretch them so they'd be in proportion with the rest of my body."

THE SAINTS

COLIN FARRELL

QUOTE

"All women have the potential to be sexy and it's nothing to do with the dress someone wears or the make-up they put on their face, it's the aged-old cliché saying: 'What comes from inside.'"

JUDE LAW

QUOTE

"Success, and even life itself, wouldn't be worth anything if I didn't have my wife and children by my side. They mean everything to me."

GERARD BUTLER

QUOTE

"Men are much more weak and vulnerable than they let on. I am full of phobias about commitment. Yet, when you break through those barriers, it's great."

KEVIN JONAS – "Kev"

QUOTE

"Even if we didn't text you till like 3:00 in the morning doesn't mean you weren't on our mind all day."

NICK JONAS – "Mr. President"

QUOTE

"My pick up line is, 'Slow down, sugar, because I'm a diabetic.'"

JOE JONAS – "DJ Danger"

QUOTE

"My favorite flirty line is, 'Hey, did you drop this?' Then you pick up a handful of sugar and say, 'It fell out of your hair.'"

THE SINNERS

KILL/MARRY/FU

MELISSA ETHERIDGE
May 29, 1961

Barbie gets a boyfriend, Ken.

ROSIE O'DONNELL
March 21, 1962

First Ford Mustang is manufactured.

1960 | 1961 | 1962 | 1963 | 1964

EDDIE MURPHY
April 3, 1961

The World Wildlife Fund founded.

WWF

Pampers introduces the first disposable diaper.

TOM CRUISE
July 3, 1962

Harvey Ball, a commercial artist, created the smiley face.

THE '60s

CYNTHIA NIXON
April 9, 1966

Star Trek television series premieres.

WOODSTOCK MUSIC & ART FAIR presents

AN AQUARIAN EXPOSITION in WHITE LAKE, N.Y.

3 DAYS of PEACE & MUSIC

WITH

AUGUST 15, 16, 17.

Woodstock music festival is held.

Neil Armstrong and Buzz Aldrin take "one small step for man, one giant leap for mankind."

1966   1967   1968   1969   **1970**

Twister sweeps the nation. Milton Bradley is accused of "selling sex in a box."

After five seasons, *The Dick Van Dyke Show* comes to end.

HUGH JACKMAN
October 12, 1968

Sesame Street premieres on the National Educational Television (NET) network.

THE **DICK VAN DYKE SHOW**

ELIZABETH TAYLOR

5'2" – 36-21-36

QUOTE

"My mother says I didn't open my eyes for eight days after I was born, but when I did, the first thing I saw was an engagement ring. I was hooked."

MARILYN MONROE

5'5½" – 37-23-36

QUOTE

"Well, whatever I am, I'm still the blonde."
- When told she was not the star in *Gentlemen Prefer Blondes*

GRACE KELLY

5'7" – 34-24-35

QUOTE

"Hollywood amuses me. Holier-than-thou for the public and unholier-than-the-devil in reality."

THE SCREEN SIRENS

THE ASSASSINATED

JOHN F. KENNEDY

Accused Assassin:
Lee Harvey Oswald

FACT

Just eight months prior to Kennedy's
assassination, Oswald tried to kill
General Edwin Walker from less
than 100 feet away as he sat at his
desk in his dining room. He missed.

JOHN LENNON

Admitted Assassin:
Mark David Chapman

FACT

Three years prior to shooting Lennon,
Chapman tried to kill himself by connecting
one end of a vacuum hose to his exhaust
pipe and the other to the inside of the car.
Unfortunately, the hose melted.

MARTIN LUTHER KING, JR

Convicted Assassin:
James Earl Ray

FACT

In a 1997 confession of his own involvement,
Lloyd Jowers said that Ray was merely a
scapegoat and that the real killer was Memphis
police officer Lt. Earl Clark. In 1999, the King
family filed suit against Jowers and he was
found liable. He was ordered to pay $100.

THE PRIMARIES

RED

FACT

Contrary to popular belief, red doesn't
make bulls angry. They are colorblind.

YELLOW

FACT

Yellow enhances concentration, which
is why it is used for legal pads.

BLUE

FACT

Studies show that weightlifters are able to
lift more weight when in a blue room.

KILL/MARRY/FU

DIANE SAWYER

Louisville, KY
Seneca High School '63

FACT
Like every other girl, she dated Warren Beatty.

KATIE COURIC

Arlington, VA
Yorktown High School '75

FACT
In 1980, then CNN president Reese Schoenfeld banned Couric from being on air after watching her fill in for an absent correspondent.

KATHIE LEE GIFFORD

Bowie, MD
Bowie High School '71

FACT
She was born the same year as Frank Gifford's oldest son, Jeff.

THE HOMECOMING

DAVID BOREANAZ

Malvern, PA
Malvern Preparatory High School '87

FACT

His father is longtime Philadelphia
weatherman, Dave Roberts.

JON HAMM

St Louis, MO
John Burroughs High School '89

FACT

Before stardom, Hamm returned to his alma
mater to teach drama. Ellie Kempler, Erin
from *The Office*, was one of his students.

RYAN SEACREST

Dunwoody, GA
Dunwoody High School '92

FACT

He originally auditioned to be one
of the judges on *American Idol*.

KILL/MARRY/FUC

MYSPACE

est. 2003 – 34 million users

FACT

I feel bad for them.

FACEBOOK

est. 2004 – 600 million users

FACT

One in every thirteen people
on the planet has an account.

TWITTER

est. 2006 – 190 million users

FACT

Five percent of users account
for 75% of all activity.

THE NETWORKS

THE NBA FINALS

est. 1947

FACT

The trophy is produced by
Tiffany & Co. each year, weighs
14.5 pounds, and is valued at $13,500.

THE STANLEY CUP

est. 1893

FACT

The cup was crafted in Sheffield,
England, and purchased for 10 guineas
(the equivalent of $48.67) in 1892.

THE WORLD SERIES

est. 1903

FACT

Called the Commissioner's Trophy,
it is the only trophy of the four
major US sports that is not named
after a particular person.

THE ROBERTS

ROBERT DE NIRO

FACT

De Niro was one of the last stars to see John Belushi alive at the Chateau Marmont. According to eyewitnesses, De Niro visited him at 3am and left minutes later after seeing that he was ill. Robin Williams stopped by as well, but had also left right away.

ROBERT DOWNEY, JR

FACT

One of Downey's closest childhood friends was Richard Hall, otherwise known as Moby. Their parents used to smoke pot together.

ROBERT PATTINSON

FACT

Pattinson skyrocketed to fame by playing vampire Edward Cullen in the *Twilight* series. According to Ancestry.com, he is an actual distant relative of Vlad the Impaler whom Bram Stoker's *Dracula* was based on.

CAMERON DIAZ
August 30, 1972

Monday Night Football debuts on ABC. The Cleveland Browns defeat the New York Jets 31-21.

HBO launches in the US.

Roe v. Wade: The US Supreme Court overturns state bans on abortion.

EVA MENDES
March 5, 1974

1970 | 1971 | 1972 | 1973 | 1974

MARK WAHLBERG
June 5, 1971

The Godfather hits theaters.

PAUL WALKER
September 12, 1973

The Rubik's Cube is invented by Hungarian architecture professor Ernő Rubik.

THE '70s

Steve Jobs and Steve Wozniak form Apple Computer Company.

So Long, Mary

After seven years, *The Mary Tyler Moore* show goes off the air.

At the age of 42, Elvis Presley dies at Graceland.

ROSARIO DAWSON
May 9, 1979

1976 · 1977 · 1978 · 1979 · **1980**

Teamsters Union president Jimmy Hoffa is reported missing.

In New York City, 'Son of Sam' shoots his first victim, beginning a crime spree that would terrorize the city for the next year.

The first *Rocky* film released

ASHTON KUTCHER
February 7, 1978

Diff'rent Strokes premieres.

Demi Guynes starts dating her first husband, songwriter, Freddy Moore. They marry in 1980, divorce in 1985. She keeps his last name.

KIL RY/FU

KHLOE KARDASHIAN

TWEET

I had blue nails last week and now I'm
in the melon shade... What's next?

KIM KARDASHIAN

TWEET

Weird Kim fact - I blow dry all my jewelry
before I put it on! I can't stand putting
on cold jewelry, it gives me the chills!

KOURTNEY KARDASHIAN

TWEET

I drive a Mercedes S class.

THE STDS

GENITAL HERPES

DEFINITION
A common sexually transmitted disease where the herpes simplex virus (HSV) enters your body through small breaks in your skin or mucous membranes and causes pain, itching, and sores in your genital area.

HOW TO GET IT
Unprotected sex, skin-to-skin contact, sex with a professional athlete.

SYMPTOMS
Pain, itching, burning sensation, small red bumps, blisters or open sores in the genital, anal, or nearby areas.

TREATMENT
There's no cure, but there are antiviral medications that can help sores heal faster, reduce frequency, and lessen the severity.

AFFTECTED AMERICANS
An estimated one out of six people between the ages of fourteen to forty-nine years old.

HIV

DEFINITION
The human immunodeficiency virus (HIV) destroys CD4 cells, a specific type of white blood cell that helps your body fight off disease. Can lead to AIDS, a chronic, potentially life-threatening condition.

HOW TO GET IT
Unprotected sex, blood transfusions, sharing needles, from mother to child.

SYMPTOMS
Many develop a brief flu-like illness two to four weeks after becoming infected but it's possible to remain symptom free for years.

TREATMENT
There is no cure, but a variety of medications can be used in combination to control the virus and slow its progression.

AFFTECTED AMERICANS
Approximately 1.1 million.

HEPATITIS B

DEFINITION
Hepatitis B is a serious liver infection caused by the hepatitis B virus (HBV). For some people, the hepatitis B infection becomes chronic, leading to liver failure, liver cancer, or cirrhosis.

HOW TO GET IT
Unprotected sex, blood transfusions, sharing needles, from mother to child.

SYMPTOMS
Abdominal pain, dark urine, joint pain, loss of appetite, vomiting, fatigue, yellowing of the skin and the whites of the eyes.

TREATMENT
There is no cure but for a chronic hepatitis B infection, there are antiviral medications that will slow down the progression.

AFFECTED AMERICANS
Approximately 4.4 million with chronic hepatitis B.

KILL/MARRY/FU

FREDDIE MERCURY

Diagnosed: 1987 – Died: 1991

FACT

Freddie liked cats. His cats were named Tom, Jerry, Tiffany, Delilah, Miko, Lily, Goliath, and Romeo. When Freddie was on tour, he would phone his cats and talk to them for hours.

JOHN HOLMES

Diagnosed: 1985 – Died: 1988

FACT

Holmes was put on trial, and ultimately acquitted, for his role in the 1982 "Wonderland Murders." The crime scene was so gruesome that detectives decided to video tape it. The video was shown in court, marking the first time in US history video was used as evidence in a criminal trial.

ARTHUR ASHE

Diagnosed: 1988 – Died: 1993

FACT

After his death, Ashe's body lay in State at the Governor's Mansion in his home state of Virginia. The last time this was allowed was for Stonewall Jackson of the Confederate Army during the Civil War.

THE INFECTED

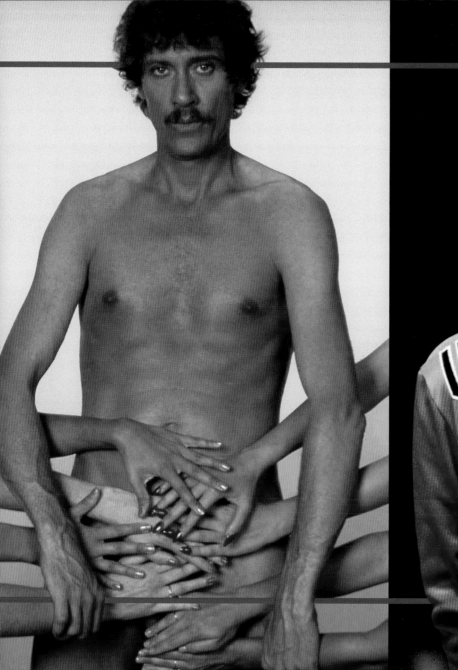

KILL/MARRY/FU

THE GUIDOS

VINNY GUADAGNINO

Seabiscuit

FACT
The dot over the letter "i" is called a tittle.

RONNIE ORTIZ-MAGRO

IFF

FACT
111111111 x 111111111 = 12345678987654321

PAUL DELVECCHIO

DJ Pauly D

FACT
Stressed is desserts spelled backwards.

KILL/MARRY/FU

JENNI FARLEY

JWOWW

FACT
Walt Disney was afraid of mice.

NICOLE POLIZZI

Snooki

FACT
Leonardo da Vinci invented the scissors.

SAMMI GIANCOLA

Sweetheart

FACT
It's impossible to lick your elbow.

THE GUIDETTES

KILL/MARRY/FU

THE GOLDEN GIRLS

DOROTHY ZBORNAK

Bea Arthur

FACT

Bea actually hated cheesecake. Throughout the show's
seven year run, the girls consumed over 100 cheesecakes.

BLANCHE DEVEREAUX

Rue McClanahan

QUOTE

"People always ask me if I'm like Blanche. And I say, 'Well,
Blanche was an oversexed, self-involved, man-crazy, vain
Southern Belle from Atlanta – and I'm not from Atlanta!'"

ROSE NYLUND

Betty White

FACT

Betty was originally cast to play the role of Blanche
and Rue was cast as Rose. When shooting the pilot, the
director suggested they switch and the rest is history.

FUN FACT
Golden Girls (originally pitched as *Miami Nice*) is one of the only
three television series where all the main characters have won
an Emmy. The other two are *All in the Family* and *Will & Grace*.

KILL/MARRY/FU

John Lennon, former Beatle and peace activist, is murdered in New York City.

MTV is launched. The first music video aired was "Video Killed The Radio Star."

ANNE HATHAWAY
November 12, 1982

Whitney Houston scores her first hit, a duet with Teddy Pendergrass called "Hold Me."

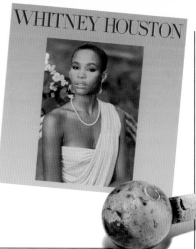
WHITNEY HOUSTON

The Crack Epidemic: crack is first introduced in the Los Angeles area and spreads like wildfire across the nation.

MTV MUSIC TELEVISION®

1980 | 1981 | 1982 | 1983 | 1984

JAKE GYLLENHAAL
December 19, 1980

JUSTIN TIMBERLAKE
January 31, 1981

Disney's Epcot Centre opens.

McDonald's introduces Chicken McNuggets.

Cabbage Patch Kids are the must-have toy for Christmas.

THE '80s

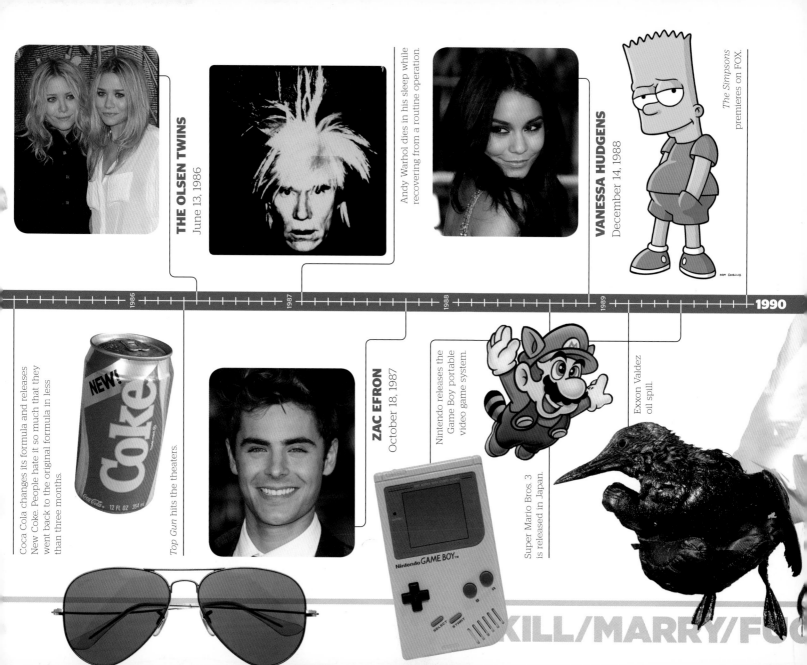

THE OLSEN TWINS
June 13, 1986

Andy Warhol dies in his sleep while recovering from a routine operation.

VANESSA HUDGENS
December 14, 1988

The Simpsons premieres on FOX.

1986   1987   1988   1989   **1990**

Coca Cola changes its formula and releases New Coke. People hate it so much that they went back to the original formula in less than three months.

Top Gun hits the theaters.

ZAC EFRON
October 18, 1987

Nintendo releases the Game Boy portable video game system.

Super Mario Bros. 3 is released in Japan.

Exxon Valdez oil spill.

NEW! Coke 12 FL OZ 354 ml

Nintendo GAME BOY™
SELECT   START

KILL/MARRY/FU

THE 27 CLUB

JIM MORRISON

The Doors

BORN	12/8/43 - Melbourne, Florida
DIED	7/3/71 - Paris, France
AGE	27
CAUSE OF DEATH	Heart failure

QUOTE

"Being drunk is a good disguise. I drink so I can talk to assholes. This includes me."

JIMI HENDRIX

The Jimi Hendrix Experience

BORN	11/27/42 - Seattle, Washington
DIED	9/18/70 - London, England
AGE	27
CAUSE OF DEATH	Asphyxiation

QUOTE

"I've been imitated so well I've heard people copy my mistakes."

KURT COBAIN

Nirvana

BORN	2/20/67 - Aberdeen, Washington
DIED	4/5/94 - Seattle, Washington
AGE	27
CAUSE OF DEATH	Shotgun wound to the head

QUOTE

"I'm gonna be a superstar musician, kill myself and go out in a flame of glory, just like Jimi Hendrix."

KILL/MARRY/FUC

THE POP TARTS

KATY PERRY

QUOTE

"If people want a role model, they can have Miley Cyrus."

RIHANNA

QUOTE

"I love the high-risk [guys]. I don't like cream puff, corny guys. Usually they are the nice guys, the ones that won't hurt you."

MILEY CYRUS

QUOTE

"I want to be Snooki, I love her. I'm obsessed. She's one of the only people I've asked for an autograph and a picture from because I love her and I'm inspired by her."

KILL/MARRY/FU

THE HOEDOWN

TAYLOR SWIFT

FACT

At twenty, she became the youngest person to win a Grammy for Album of the Year. Alanis Morissette was twenty-one.

CARRIE UNDERWOOD

FACT

During her *American Idol* audition, she revealed that she had her third nipple removed.

JULIANNE HOUGH

FACT

When they were kids, she was in a pop trio with Mark Ballas and her brother Derek called 2B1G (2 Boys 1 Girl).

OTIS REDDING - December 10, 1967

Redding's plane crashed following a performance in Cleveland, Ohio. Seven of the eight people on board died. Redding was only twenty-six years old. Fortunately, he had recorded "(Sittin' On) The Dock of the Bay" three days prior. He considered it unfinished, having whistled one of the verses he was planning to write lyrics for later.

MARVIN GAYE - April 1, 1984

Following a 1983 tour plagued with bouts of depression and the return of his drug addiction, Gaye moved in with his parents in an attempt to get his life together. The day before his 45th birthday he got in a fight with his father. The fight ended when his father shot him twice in the chest. He pled guilty to voluntary manslaughter and was sentenced to five years probation.

SAM COOKE - December 11, 1964

Cooke met Elisa Boyer at a nightclub and took her back to an LA motel room. Boyer claimed he was going to rape her so while he was in the bathroom, she grabbed her things to leave, taking his wallet and most of his clothing by mistake. When Cooke came out to find his things missing, he ran out of the room wearing nothing but his shoes and a sports jacket. He broke into the manager's office where he thought Boyer was hiding. The manager, Bertha Franklin, shot and killed him. Cooke was only thirty-three years old. The killing was ruled a justifiable homicide and Boyer was arrested for prostitution shortly thereafter in an unrelated case.

THE SOULS

KILL/MARRY/FU

THE SPITTERS

LIL WAYNE

Dwayne Michael Carter, Jr

FACT

Lil Wayne once dated *Video Vixen* Karrine Steffans, also known as "Superhead." She said they were in love and that "Wayne's my John Lennon, I'm his Yoko Ono." Indeed, she was the inspiration behind his song, "Prostitute Flange."

EMINEM

Marshall Bruce Mathers III

FACT

Eminem's mother filed a $10 million slander suit against her son for lyrics in his debut single, "My Name Is," claiming that she suffered emotional distress, sleepless nights, damage to her credit rating, and loss of her mobile home. The case was settled for $25,000 - $23,354 of which went to her attorney.

KANYE WEST

Kanye Omari West

FACT

Kanye financed his "Through the Wire" video, inspired by his near fatal car crash, out of his own pocket, and submitted the video to BET and MTV himself. He told *Time* magazine, "Death is the best thing that can ever happen to a rapper. Almost dying isn't bad either."

KILL/MARRY/FUC

JENNA JAMESON

FACT

Opened in Edison, NJ, in 2006, Jameson was one of the first stars to have a brick laid in her honor on the Adult Star Path of Fame.

TERA PATRICK

FACT

Pre-porn, she was a registered nurse and earned a degree in microbiology from Boise State University.

SASHA GREY

FACT

Marina Ann Hantzis' stage name was inspired by Oscar Wilde's novel *The Picture of Dorian Gray*. The name "Sasha" was taken from Sascha Konietzko, the frontman of German industrial rock band KMFDM.

THE SWALLOWERS

THE DIC

JOSEPH STALIN

Russian Dictator

YEARS IN POWER
1924-1953

ESTIMATED DEATH TOLL
60 million

FACT
Tried to make super warriors for his
army by breeding humans with apes.

ADOLF HITLER

German Dictator

YEARS IN POWER
1933-1945

ESTIMATED DEATH TOLL
12 million

FACT
Was monorchic, which means he
only had one ball. He also had syphilis.

MAO TSE-TUNG

Chinese Dictator

YEARS IN POWER
1945-1976

ESTIMATED DEATH TOLL
70 million

FACT
Had green teeth because he chewed
on green tea leaves instead of brushing.

KILL/MARRY/FUC

THE PROTEINS

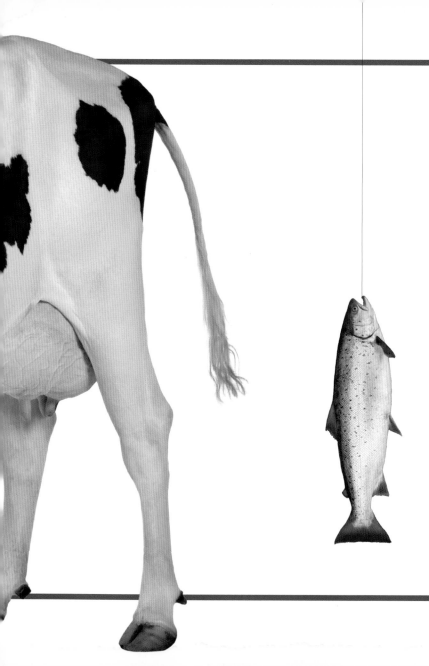

CHICKEN

....

Which came first?

FACT

A chicken with red earlobes will produce brown eggs, and a chicken with white earlobes will produce white eggs. The color of the shell is the only difference between the two.

BEEF

....

It's what for dinner.

FACT

The average lifespan of a cow is 22 years, assuming they could avoid the slaughterhouse. Otherwise, it's 4. The oldest cow ever recorded was Big Bertha who died at age 48 in 1993.

FISH

....

Plenty of em' in the sea!

FACT

There are more species of fish than all species of mammals, reptiles, amphibians, and birds combined.

KRISTEN STEWART
April 9, 1990

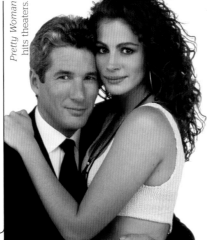

Pretty Woman hits theaters.

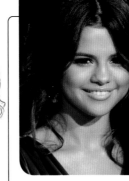

SELENA GOMEZ
July 22, 1992

O.J. Simpson completes the KMF trifecta.

1990 1991 1992 1993 1994

LIAM HEMSWORTH
January 13, 1990

Sega's first Sonic the Hedgehog game is released to rival Mario, Nintendo's flagship character.

Tim Berners-Lee and Robert Cailliau launch the World Wide Web.

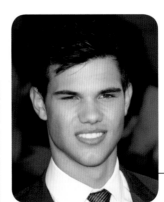

TAYLOR LAUTNER
February 11, 1992

Jurassic Park released, regarded as a landmark in the use of computer-generated imagery.

THE '90s

TAYLOR MOMSEN
July 26, 1993

1996

JUSTIN BIEBER
March 1, 1994

THE END

RUTH SNYDER'S DEATH PICTURED!—This is perhaps the most remarkable exclusive picture in the history of criminology. It shows the actual scene in the Sing Sing death house as the lethal current surged through Ruth Snyder's body at 11:06 last night. Her helmeted head is stiffened in death, her face masked and an electrode strapped to her bare right leg. The autopsy table on which her body was removed is beside her. Judd Gray, mumbling a prayer, followed her down the narrow corridor at 11:14. "Father, forgive them, for they don't know what they are doing!" were Ruth's last words. The picture is the first Sing Sing execution picture and the first of a woman's electrocution. *Story p. 3; other pics, 8-10 back pages.*

FIRING SQUAD

FACT

After being granted his last wish to watch the *Lord of the Rings* trilogy, Ronnie Lee Gardner was executed by firing squad in Utah in 2010. Five anonymous gunmen, with four bullets and one blank, shot at a target on Gardner's heart as he sat strapped to a chair in a small room.

HANGING

FACT

Billy Bailey was the last person to be hanged in the US. The hanging took place in Delaware in 1996. The only states that still have hanging as an option are Washington and New Hampshire.

ELECTRIC CHAIR

FACT

Thomas Howard, a reporter for the *Daily News*, snuck a camera in to the 1928 execution of Ruth Snyder and took a picture right as she was being electrocuted. It marked the first and last time a picture has been taken during an execution and is considered to be the first tabloid photo. Howard was promoted and eventually went on to become head of photography at the White House. His grandson is *Cheers* star George Wendt and his great grandson is SNL actor, Jason Sudeikis.

KILL/MARRY/FU

THE BLONDES:
Charlize Theron: WENN.com
Scarlett Johansson: Allstar/Graham Whitby Boot
Blake Lively: Greg Allen/Rex USA

THE BRUNETTES:
Angelina Jolie, Megan Fox: WENN.com
Mila Kunis: Allstar/Graham Whitby Boot

THE GINGERS:
Danny Bonaduce: Peter Brooker/Rex USA
Carrot Top: Ray Filmano/WENN.com
David Caruso: www.xsubs.tv

THE CITIES:
Chicago, Los Angeles: iStockphoto.com/photo168
New York: iStockphoto.com/chrisp0

THE CLASS OF '93:
Seth Poppel/Yearbook Library

THE THREE OF SPADE:
Pamela Anderson: Jody Cortes/WENN.com
Carmen Electra: Fabrizio Picco/WENN.com
Heather Locklear: Peter Brooker/Rex USA
Pamela Anderson & David Spade: Getty Images
Carmen Electra & David Spade:
Timothy Jackson/WENN.com
Heather Locklear & David Spade:
Gabo/Chris/Bauer-Griffin.com

THE '20s:
Betty White, Barbara Walters, Cloris Leachman,
Hugh Hefner, Joe Jackson:
Allstar/Graham Whitby Boot
Bob Barker: FayesVision/WENN.com
Toast: iStockphoto.com/nexusseven
Toaster: iStockphoto.com/pixhook
TV: iStockphoto.com/Spiderstock
Sunglasses: iStockphoto.com/empire331
King Tut: www.kingtutdublin.ie
The Kid poster, Einstein, Babe Ruth, Chanel No. 5:
http://commons.wikimedia.org
Winnie the Pooh: Image.net, jperry

THE HAPPY HOUR:
Wine: iStockphoto.com/ailan
Liquor: iStockphoto.com/fotojagodka
Wine: iStockphoto.com/artJazz

THE CURSED:
Reese Witherspoon: Nikki Nelson/WENN.com
Kate Winslet, Sandra Bullock: Apega/WENN.com
Reese Witherspoon & Ryan Phillippe:
Nikki Nelson/WENN.com
Kate Winselt & Sam Mendes:
Allstar/Graham Whitby Boot
Sandra Bullock & Jesse James: WENN.com
Red carpet: iStockphoto.com/matejmm
Gold frame #1: iStockphoto.com/macniak
Gold frame #2: iStockphoto.com/Photo2008
Gold frame #3: iStockphoto.com/NinaMalyna

THE ROMANTICS:
Chris Brown, John Mayer: Jim Smeal/BEImages
Ben Roethlisberger: Judy Eddy/WENN.com

THE ONE NIGHT STAND:
Lindsay Lohan, Britney Spears, Paris Hilton:
BEN/GABO/DEAN/BAUER-GRIFFIN

THE IVY LEAGUE:
Amanda Peet: Erik Pendzich/Rex USA
Natalie Portman: Camilla Morandi/Rex USA
Rashida Jones: Matt Baron/BEImages
Matthew Fox, James Franco: HRC/WENN.com
John Krasinski: Apega/WENN.com

THE STONERS:
Illustrated by Mat Bartlett - www.matbartlett.co.uk

THE '30s:
Debbie Reynolds, Robert Redford: WENN.com
Sophia Loren, Jane Fonda, Warren Beatty,
Sean Connery: Allstar/Graham Whitby Boot
Beer: iStockphoto.com/OliverChilds
Cookie: iStockphoto.com/burwellphotography
Nylons: iStockphoto.com/Opla

Chocolate doughnut: iStockphoto.com/spaxiax
Doughnut with bite: iStockphoto.com/klikk
Glazed Doughnut: iStockphoto.com/kone
Pink Doughnut: Shutterstock.com/ChrisLeachman
Gone with the Wind: Allstar/MGM
Quarter: iStockphoto.com/Gaussian_Blur
Al Capone, Frankenstein:
http://commons.wikimedia.org
Scotch tape: www.etsy.com
Donald Duck: wwwworldsofdisney07.proboards.com
Monopoly dog: www.worldofmonopoly.com

THE MOVERS:
Steve Jobs: Ray Tang/Rex USA
Mark Zuckerberg: AP Photo/Paul Sakuma
Bill Gates: Dominic Chan/WENN.com
Racecar: iStockphoto.com/pronkgraphics

THE SHAKERS:
Michael J. Fox: Tommy Gravad/WENN.com
Muhammad Ali: Michael Carpenter/WENN.com
Ozzy Osbourne: WENN.com

THE JENNIFERS:
Jennifer Lopez, Jennifer Garner:
Allstar/Graham Whitby Boot
Jennifer Aniston: WENN.com

THE OCEAN'S THREE:
Matt Damon, Brad Pitt, George Clooney:
http://tinyurl.com/3n8z39m

THE PRIORITIES/THE FIRSTS:
Heart: Andrei Calangiu/Dreamstime.com
Money: iStockphoto.com/Kativ
Condom: Shutterstock.com/robybret
First Love, First Kiss, First Time:
iStockphoto.com/bubaone

THE '40s:
Barbra Streisand, Bette Midler, Cher:
Allstar/Graham Whitby Boot
Martin Scorcese, George Lucas: Allstar/David Gadd
Steven Spielberg: Allstar/Kurt Kreiger

Alien: iStockphoto.com/Shiva3d
Slinky: iStockphoto.com/evemilla
Helmet: Shutterstock.com/titelio
Citizen Kane poster: Allstar/RKO
Spaceship: iStockphoto.com/ZargonDesign
Anne Frank: Everett Collection/Rex USA
McDonald's: www.aboutmcdonalds.com
Bugs Bunny: www.turnertapkit.com
Oscar: http://goodfilmguide.co.uk
Scrabble letters: www.fuzzimo.com

THE RYANS:
Ryan Gosling: J. Arbeit/WENN.com
Ryan Phillippe: Anita Bugge/WENN.com
Ryan Reynolds: Dominic Chan/WENN.com

THE BAD DRIVERS:
Halle Berry, Rebecca Gayheart: WENN.com
Brandy Norwood: Judy Eddy/WENN.com

THE CANDY:
Milky Way, Snickers, 3 Musketeers, M&M's, Skittles,
Reese's Pieces: http://commons.wikimedia.org/
User: Evan-Amos/Food
http://www.flickr.com/photos/30348074@N00
Individual pieces of candy: Sebastien Roche-Lochen

THE CHAINS:
Applebees: http://cozinhadosbrothers.blogspot.com
Olive Garden: http://multivu.prnewswire.com
Red Lobster: www.redlobster.com
McDonald's: iStockphoto.com/GeorgeClerk
Wendy's: iStockphoto.com/toddmedia
Burger King: iStockphoto.com/ermingut

THE CRITTERS:
Cockroach: iStockphoto.com/Jgroup
Worms: iStockphoto.com/Zoediak
Spider: iStockphoto.com/Antagain

THE QUITTERS:
Mackenzie Phillips: WENN.com
Janice Dickinson: Peter Brooker/Rex USA
Heidi Fleiss: Patrick Rideaux/Rex USA

THE CREDITS

THE '50s:
Christie Brinkley, Sharon Stone: WENN.com
Michelle Pfeiffer: Allstar/Tim Matthews
Pierce Brosnan: Allstar/Graham Whitby Boot
Mel Gibson: Adriana M. Barraza/WENN.com
Alec Baldwin: Ivan Nikolov/WENN.com
Shirley Temple: Allstar/Cinetext/Allstar Collection
James Dean: Allstar/Warner Bros.
Baseball: iStockphoto.com/anplett
KFC bucket: www.westgatefitness.ca
The Catcher in the Rye:
www.manhattanrarebooks-literature.com
Playboy: http://en.wikipedia.org
Mr. Potato Head: http://healthland.time.com
Charlie Brown: http://blogs.courant.com

THE TALK TITANS:
Illustrated by Mat Bartlett - www.matbartlett.co.uk

THE CONDIMENTS/THE UTENSILS:
Mustard, Mayo, and Ketchup bottles, blobs of
mustard and ketchup: iStockphoto.com/thebroker
Blob of mayo: Shutterstock.com/Valentyn Volkov
Knife, fork, spoon: iStockphoto.com/bluestocking

THE JESSICAS:
Jessica Alba, Jessica Biel: Allstar/Graham Whitby Boot
Jessica Simpson: WENN.com

THE SAINTS:
Colin Farrell, Jude Law, Gerard Butler: WENN.com

THE SINNERS:
The Jonas Brothers: Focus Pictures/WENN.com

THE '60s:
Melissa Etheridge, Hugh Jackman:
Allstar/Graham Whitby Boot
Rosie O'Donnell: Joseph Marzullo/WENN.com
Cynthia Nixon: Allstar/Neil Tingle
Eddie Murphy: James McCauley/Rex USA
Tom Cruise: FayesVision/WENN.com
Moon: iStockphoto.com/CarolinaSmith
Baby: iStockphoto.com/tarinoel

Smiley Face: iStockphoto.com/DSGpro
Ford Mustang: iStockphoto.com/StanRohrer
'60s TV: iStockphoto.com/jgroup
Malcom X, Woodstock poster: http://en.wikipedia.org
Ken doll: http://blogs.sun-sentinel.com
Captain Kirk and Spock: www.highdefdiscnews.com
Bert and Ernie: http://img55.imageshack.us/
img55/1407/bert20and20ernie.jpg

THE SCREEN SIRENS:
Elizabeth Taylor: SNAP/Rex/Rex USA
Marilyn Monroe: Michale Ochs Archives
via Getty Images
Grace Kelly: Cinetext/Allstar Collection

THE ASSASSINATED:
John F. Kennedy: Allstar Collection
John Lennon: PR Photo/WENN.com
Martin Luther King, Jr.:
CSU Archives/Everett Collection/Rex USA
Lee Harvey Oswald: http://commons.wikimedia.org
Mark David Chapman: http://en.wikipedia.org
James Earl Ray: www.noga.co.il

THE PRIMARIES:
Red, Yellow, Blue: iStockphoto.com/Monkie

THE HOMECOMING:
Seth Poppel/Yearbook Library

THE NETWORKS/THE SERIES:
Larry O'Brien trophy: http://commons.wikimedia.org
Stanley Cup: www.tjpro.com/stanley.htm
Commissioner's Trophy: www.fmnh.org

THE ROBERTS:
Robert De Niro, Robert Downey, Jr.,
Robert Pattinson: WENN.com

THE '70s:
Cameron Diaz, Rosario Dawson, Mark Wahlberg,
Paul Walker: Allstar/Graham Whitby Boot
Eva Mendes: Apega/WENN.com
Ashton Kutcher: A. Miller/WENN.com

Demi Moore: Everett Collection/Rex USA
Football: iStockphoto.com/ spxChrome
Wire hanger: iStockphoto.com/ElisaGH
Rocky: Everett Collection/Rex USA
Gary Coleman: Allstar Collection
Toilet: iStockphoto.com/aguirre_mar
Rubik's cube: richardnewmansays.blogspot.com
TV Guide: www.sitcomsonline.com

THE KARDASHIANS:
http://br.eonline.com

THE INFECTED:
Freddie Mercury: Fraser Gray/Rex USA
John Holmes: Kenji
Arthur Ashe: Richard Conricus/Rex USA

THE GUIDOS & THE GUIDETTES:
Vinne Guadagnino, Ronnie Ortiz-Magro,
Paul DelVecchio, Jenni Farley, Nicole Polizzi,
Sammi Giancola: http://mtvpress.com

THE GOLDEN GIRLS:
The Golden Girls: ABC Studios via Getty Images

THE '80s:
Anne Hathaway: WENN.com
The Olsen twins: Michael Carpenter/WENN.com
Vanessa Hudgens, Jake Gyllenhaal, Zac Efron:
Allstar/Graham Whitby Boot
Justin Timberlake: Allstar/Tim Matthews
Beetle: Shutterstock.com/Ivaschenko Roman
Crack Pipe: iStockphoto.com/KarenMower
Oil bird: Eric Vidal/Rex USA
Cabbage Patch Kid: www.powerhousemuseum.com
Epcot Center: http://wikitravel.org/en/Epcot
Ray Ban Sunglasses: iStockphoto.com/Crisma
Andy Warhol: www.warhol.org/pressroom
McNuggets: www.aboutmcdonalds.com

THE 27 CLUB:
Jim Morrison: Alan Messer/Rex USA
Jimi Hendrix: Marc Sharratt/Rex USA
Kurt Cobain: Everett Collection/Rex USA

THE POP TARTS:
Katy Perry, Rihanna, Miley Cyrus: WENN.com

THE HOEDOWN:
Taylor Swift, Julianne Hough: Jim Smeal/BEImages
Carrie Underwood: WENN.com

THE SOULS:
Sam Cooke: Michael Ochs Archives/Getty Images
Otis Redding: Everett Collection/Rex USA
Marvin Gaye: Dezo Hoffmann/Rex USA

THE SPITTERS:
Lil Wayne, Eminem: WENN.com
Kanye West: Ed Jones/Rex USA

THE SWALLOWERS:
Jenna Jameson: www.clubjenna.com
Tera Patrick: www.terapatrick.com
Sasha Grey: www.deepthroatlove.com

THE DICS:
Illustrated by Mat Bartlett - www.matbartlett.co.uk

THE PROTEINS:
Chicken: Shutterstock.com/Selena
Cow: Shutterstock.com/EricIsselée
Fish: Shutterstock.com/Krasowit

THE '90s:
Selena Gomez: WENN.com
Kristen Stewart, Liam Hemsworth, Taylor Lautner,
Justin Beiber: Allstar/Graham Whitby Boot
Taylor Momsen: Will Alexander/WENN.com
T-Rex: iStockphoto.com/JoeLena
OJ & Nicole Brown Simpson: BEImages
Pretty Woman: www.imisstheoldschool.com
Sonic the Hedgehog: www.rankopedia.com

THE END:
Noose: iStockphoto.com/claylib
Blank paper: iStockphoto.com/pierredesvarre
Ruth Snyder: NY Daily News via Getty Images

Born and raised in Wilmington, DE, I was an insomniac child obsessed with Nick at Nite. I moved to Los Angeles when I was seventeen to go to Loyola Marymount University and pursue a career in TV production. I kind of wanted to be like Sally from *The Dick Van Dyke Show* but a little less tragic. I worked at a batting cage throughout college and after graduation, I used up all my connections to get my first real TV job on *8 Simple Rules for Dating My Teenage Daughter,* but right before I was about to start, John Ritter died and kind of threw a wrench in my plans. I ended up taking a job at *Entertainment Tonight* and ultimately *The Insider* where I spent the next seven years working with awesome people, learning the ins and outs of the entertainment industry but also dying a slow pop culture infused death. Two years ago, I decided to make this book and then got laid off just in time to actually write it.

THE BIO

I love my mom. A lot. Thank you Nora Huber for giving birth and everything else.

Huge thanks to Damian Browning for designing this book and believing in it in the first place. We've never met, we've never even talked on the phone, but from across the pond and in a little under 2,000 emails (I counted) we made a book! I couldn't have asked for a better designer to work with and I feel bad that he actually had to type this text in himself instead of reading it when the book came out but that's just proof that I literally could not have done this without him.

Thank you to Pat O'Brien for inspiration and to Josh Lopour, Lindsay Bonsall, and Joni from FedEx Office for helping me to make it happen. Thank you to my gambling problem for teaching me how to take risks and for making me broke enough to take some bigger ones. Thanks to Mark Batty for seeing potential and to Buzz Poole, Christopher D Salyers, and Eli Stockwell for seeing me through this process. Thank you to Dan Huber for being an awesome brother, Joan Teitelman for being kind, Jill Nelson for being helpful, Sebastien Roche-Lochen for doing me a favor, and Mat Bartlett for being awesome and talented. Thank you to Aaron Null, Brianne Allen, Tim Cyrol, JP Richards, Joe Lucas, Dave Heikka, Matt Smith, Sharon Hashimoto, Delleon Weins, Walter Blatt, Sarah Weir, Ken O'Hanlon (not so much), Kara Grugan, Pat Grugan, Kate Trzaskos, my awesome book club, and everyone else who helped me out and offered nothing but encouragement. Last but not least, thank you to my grandfather for not making me get into too much detail whenever he would ask what my book was about.

For more fun and to download the KMF app, go to **killmarryfuc.com**!

THE THANKS   **KILL/MARRY/FUC**